Picture This!

Written by Nicola Belsham

Contents	Page
Chapter 1. *What A Cool Job!*	4
Chapter 2. *Illustrate To Communicate*	8
Chapter 3. *From Scribble To Picture*	10
Photo Feature: *The Illustration Studio*	14
Chapter 4. *Complete Composition*	18
Chapter 5. *Fabulous Final Art*	24
Index And Bookweb Links	32
Glossary	Inside Back Cover

Chapter Snapshots

1. What A Cool Job! Page 4
What could be better than drawing pictures for a job? But there's a lot more to it than meets the eye . . .

2. Illustrate To Communicate Page 8
It's important to choose the right illustrator for each project. But with all the different styles and techniques, how do you decide?

3. From Scribble To Picture
Page 10
Which picture goes where? What should it show? How big should it be? What is the deadline? How much will I be paid?

"In my studio, the
I would like to

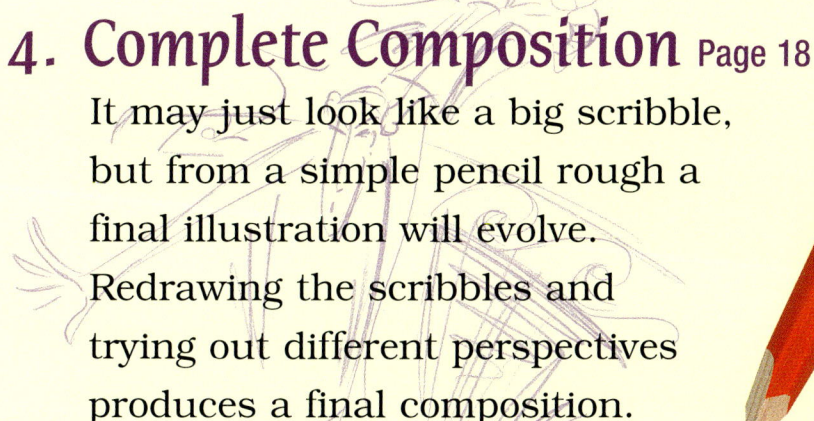

4. Complete Composition Page 18

It may just look like a big scribble, but from a simple pencil rough a final illustration will evolve. Redrawing the scribbles and trying out different perspectives produces a final composition.

5. Fabulous Final Art
Page 24

The fun stage! Let's see how all those pencil drawings are transformed into the final illustration. I must work quickly though—there is still much to do if I am to meet the deadline!

phone rings and I am asked if illustrate the book. I say yes!"

1. What A Cool Job!

We have probably never met, although you may recognize my name. My work is seen by many people each day, and yet they do not know me.

Let me introduce myself—I'm an illustrator. This means that my job is to draw pictures. Drawing pictures for a job? "What a cool job!" you say.

Well, it is a great job, but there's a lot more to it than just drawing pictures. First of all, someone has to *want* me to draw their pictures.

I have to show that I can draw in a style and technique that suits the project they have in mind. The illustration must include everything that my client wants and I need to complete it by a certain date.

Which Style To Choose?

Illustrators work in different styles. A style is how an illustrator interprets and presents what they see or want to show. One illustrator might draw a cat realistically while another illustrator might draw the same cat as a cartoon. Both are good illustrations, as they are both an interpretation of the cat. They are just different styles. Choosing a style for an illustration often depends on how you want the illustration to look, or the emotion you want your illustration to show.

Technique

Technique is the way an illustrator uses tools to produce his or her illustration. For example, the illustrator who drew the realistic cat might have used a pencil in fine strokes to give a feeling of soft, warm fur. The other illustrator might have used colorful paint in large, broad brush strokes to show a feeling of movement as the cat leaps through the air. With all the different types of paints, pastels, pens, pencils, markers, chalks, and brushes that illustrators can use and all the different ways illustrators can use them, choosing an illustrator can be a tough decision!

I have a portfolio, a folder that showcases my best work. I want my client to choose me for the job because they think that I am the best person for it!

What's A Portfolio?

Illustrators obtain work by showing their portfolios to the people and companies for whom they want to work. A portfolio is like a photo album. Portfolios show the many styles and techniques that the illustrator can use.

2. Illustrate To Communicate

Everyone loves books, and everyone has their favorite story books. Perhaps you even have a favorite illustrator. But how did the illustrations get in the book? How did they develop? Where did they start? Were lines drawn first, or were ideas formed first? Or was the illustrator told what to draw by someone else?

Often, it's a combination of all of these things. When people create a leaflet, a poster, or a book, they may decide to have it illustrated. The illustrations are used to visually communicate the information in the text.

Communication In Our Everyday Environment

Illustrations on posters and leaflets often provide a lot of information. This is because people walking past a poster do not always have time to stop and read it, but they remember the picture or illustration. So illustrations are tools used to communicate.

Symbols are especially useful. Symbols are pictures that stand for ideas. A symbol on a traffic light lets us know when it is OK to cross the road. A symbol on a drink bottle tells us that the bottle can be recycled.

How many symbols did you see on the way to school today?

Let's imagine that you are publishing a book. First, you read the story. If the story is serious, you will want realistic pictures to convey its mood. If your story is funny, you might want a cartoon style to add extra humor to the story.

Once you have decided on the style of pictures, you call the illustrator.

The client, having made her decision on style, calls the illustrator.

3. From Scribble To Picture

For the Bookweb story, *Understudies*, the publisher decides that a humorous style of illustration is best. The story is about a ballet performance that does not go as planned, so a feeling of movement would also be good in the illustrations. The publisher looks through the portfolios of several different illustrators. They choose me!

In my studio, the phone rings and I am asked if I would like to illustrate the book. I say yes! The publisher sends me a layout and a document called an illustration brief.

I check my calendar to make sure I can do the job in the time specified by the brief.

The layout shows me the spaces available for the illustrations and where the text is going to be placed. It is important that my illustrations fit into these spaces and do not cross into the text.

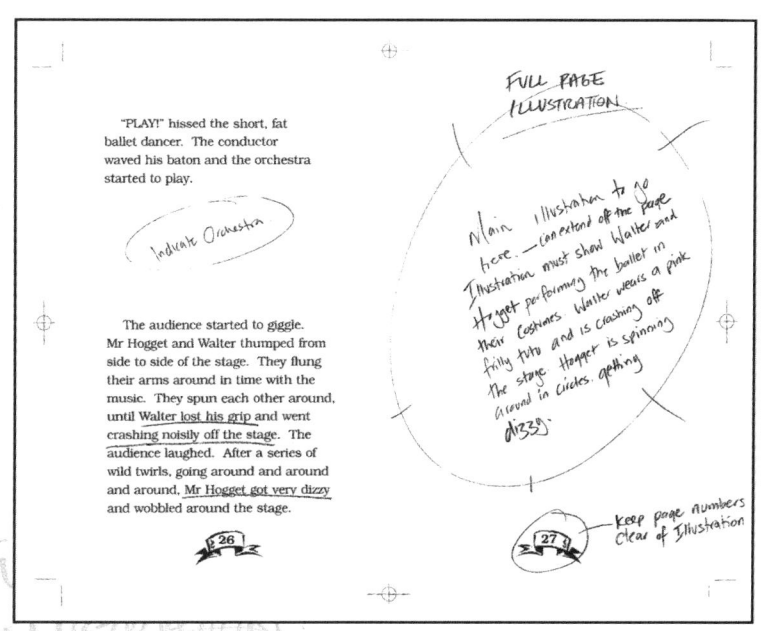

The illustration brief describes what must appear in each illustration.

Attached to the brief is a contract, a document that lets me know the date the illustrations need to be finished and how much I will be paid for the job. It is very important to fulfill all the requirements of the brief by the deadline date if I am to be paid. Often, I have several different projects to work on, so I check my calendar to make sure that I can complete the job by the deadline. I want to be sure that I can complete the job to the best of my ability!

The next stage is to start work on some pencil roughs. I read the story and brief. I start to think about the characters. Who are they? What are their personalities? What might they look like?

After reading the story and becoming familiar with the characters, I decide to make Mr. Hogget small and round—like a "hog," as his name suggests. As the owner of a theater, he is probably quite wealthy, so I always draw him wearing a suit. His personality is confident and determined, and he is often exclaiming or shouting. So I color his suit bright red.

Walter, his assistant, is usually a little nervous and often fumbling around Mr. Hogget. The text says that he is tall and thin, so I decide to make him *really* tall and thin so that there will be an obvious contrast between the two characters.

The Illustration Studio
Illustrators work in a studio and need a lot of equipment to produce their illustrations. Here are just some of the basic tools that an illustrator uses.

Safety

Illustrators need to take care when using certain materials and tools. Sharp knives and scalpels may cause serious injury if they are not used safely. Many paints, glues, and markers also give off fumes that can be dangerous to breathe!

Once the characters have been designed, I proceed with my pencil roughs. I start scribbling, letting my pencil transfer my thoughts to paper. I don't worry about lines in the wrong place or whether hands and faces are drawn correctly. I don't even use my eraser. I am concentrating on drawing all of the elements into the space available to create a good composition.

A Matter Of Composition

Composition describes how all the elements within a painting or illustration look and how the shapes fit together on the page.

During the 1300s, artists developed special rules and mathematical diagrams to describe what made a good composition. Those rules still work today.

Basically, a good composition is one that looks pleasing to the eye. For example, if an illustration shows a person with a house in the background, it would be a good idea to put your person to one side of the picture.

This looks better than placing the person right in the center of the picture.

Often, artists and illustrators try out a variety of compositions before they decide on one that best shows all the elements of the illustration in a comfortable and pleasing way.

I try out different poses for each character until I draw something that looks right. To anyone else it just looks like a big scribble!

4. Complete Composition

When I have chosen a good composition from my scribbles, I redraw my illustration, concentrating on making the shapes more accurate. People often say to me that they can't draw, but I don't think this is true. Everyone can draw, they just have different drawing styles.

The way I draw Walter's face in this illustration is completely different than how someone else might draw it. This doesn't make one illustration good and one bad—it's just a matter of style.

As I draw Walter's face, I try to imagine how he might be feeling. He has just fallen down, so his face is scrunched up in discomfort. Why has he fallen? Perhaps his long legs have become tangled. I spend some time working out how his feet should look, tangled together, and on the perspective of his fall.

What Is Perspective?

Perspective describes how we show a three-dimensional object on a two-dimensional surface. Perspective usually consists of one or more vanishing points, which lie on the horizon of a picture. They help to describe the object in three dimensions.

The vanishing point creates depth and appears where parallel lines in the picture seem to meet. For example, Cube A has no vanishing points. It appears flat on the picture surface. A picture like this is called two-dimensional.

Cube B has one vanishing point. All of the lines meet at the same point which is at the horizon.

Cube C has two vanishing points. Both points are at the horizon. Seeing more than just one side of Cubes B and C makes them appear three-dimensional on the picture surface, and this creates a feeling of distance. This distance is shown by Cubes D and E.

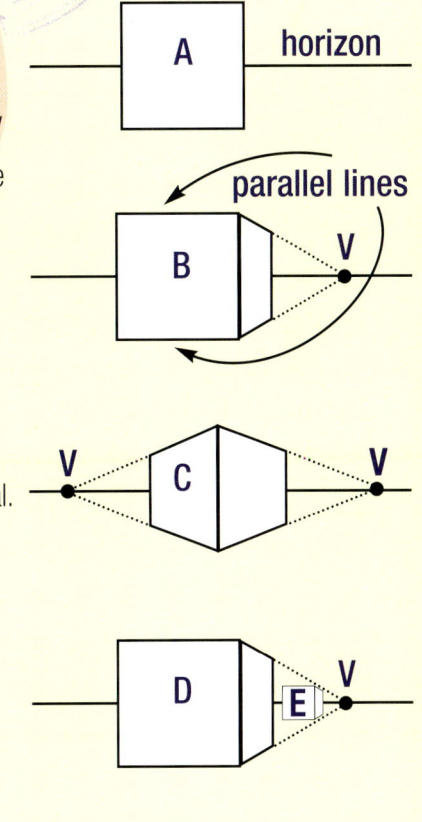

Let's look at page 27 of the story *Understudies* in Bookweb 4. Mr. Hogget, the theater owner, and Walter, his assistant, are trying to perform a ballet dance. The illustration shows Walter crashing noisily off the stage while Mr. Hogget is getting very dizzy and wobbling around the stage. During this scene, I need to show that an orchestra is playing while all this action is happening.

The perspective in this illustration shows a front view of Walter, arms outstretched in the foreground and legs tangled behind. We are looking at the scene from above.

I decide that Walter's act of falling is funnier and of more interest to the illustration than Mr. Hogget's spinning around, getting dizzy. As a result, Walter dominates the illustration by being in the foreground, and Mr. Hogget balances the image in the background. Drawing Mr. Hogget very small in size compared with Walter adds to the feeling of depth and perspective because it looks as if he is further away.

Finally, I add musical notes to show the orchestra playing along with the action.

When I am happy with my pencil roughs, I fax them to the publisher. I hope my client likes them, too!

Sometimes, the client sends a fax requesting changes to some parts of the pencil roughs. The client is spending a lot of money on the illustrations, so he or she needs to be sure that the illustrations are exactly right. This is why I always send pencil roughs first. I wouldn't want to make changes once the full-color illustrations are complete!

Fax Machines

The word "fax" is short for "facsimile," which means "exact copy." In 1866, the world's first fax machine was invented by an Italian physicist named Giovanni Caselli. Facsimiles were used mainly by newspaper offices to send photographs. However, during the 1980s, fax machines became popular in many other types of businesses.

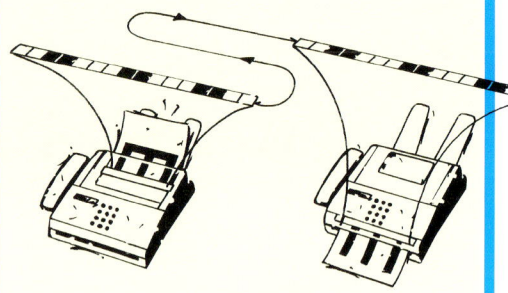

A fax machine sends information by scanning the light and dark areas of a page and changing them into electrical signals. These signals travel down the phone line to the receiving fax machine. The receiving fax then changes the electronic signals back into a pattern of light and dark areas.

On this rough, I am asked to change Mr. Hogget's trousers to tight shorts. I agree that this is a good change, as it will make the illustration funnier.

(Before)

(After)

I fax the revised illustration rough back to the client. Now I wait for the publisher's approval!

5. Fabulous Final Art

Hooray! The publisher is happy and has approved my pencil roughs. Now it is time to start the final illustrations. This is the really fun part.

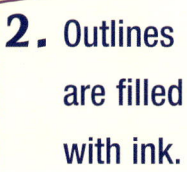

1. The sketches are traced.

First, I trace all of my pencil roughs onto a special art board called scratch board. I do this using carbon paper.

When my tracing is complete, I fill in all the outlines with ink. The scratch board means I can paint on the lines, and using a special tool, scratch into them or scratch them out completely if I make a mistake. This technique helps to give the illustration a feeling of movement.

2. Outlines are filled with ink.

I spend a lot of time carefully matching the tracing to my pencil roughs. It is important not to leave anything out now that the roughs have been approved!

3. Additional lines for movement are added.

Once the outlines are complete, I photocopy them onto watercolor paper. Watercolor paper is special paper that you soak and stick to a board using a gummed tape. As the paper dries, it stretches.

4. Outlines are copied onto watercolor paper and soaked.

Have you ever painted onto paper only to have it buckle up as it dries? It's very annoying! Stretching watercolor paper means this won't happen.

5. The paper is stretched, ready for coloring.

The Color Wheel

The many colors that we see every day can be made from just three colors which are called primary colors. These are yellow, red, and blue. We mix these colors together to create secondary colors. Secondary colors are orange, green, and purple.

Monochromatic colors are a set of colors located in the same part of the wheel. For example, the set of colors yellow, yellow-orange, orange, and orange-red make a monochrome.

Complementary colors are the colors on the opposite side of the wheel. Blue is the complementary color of orange.

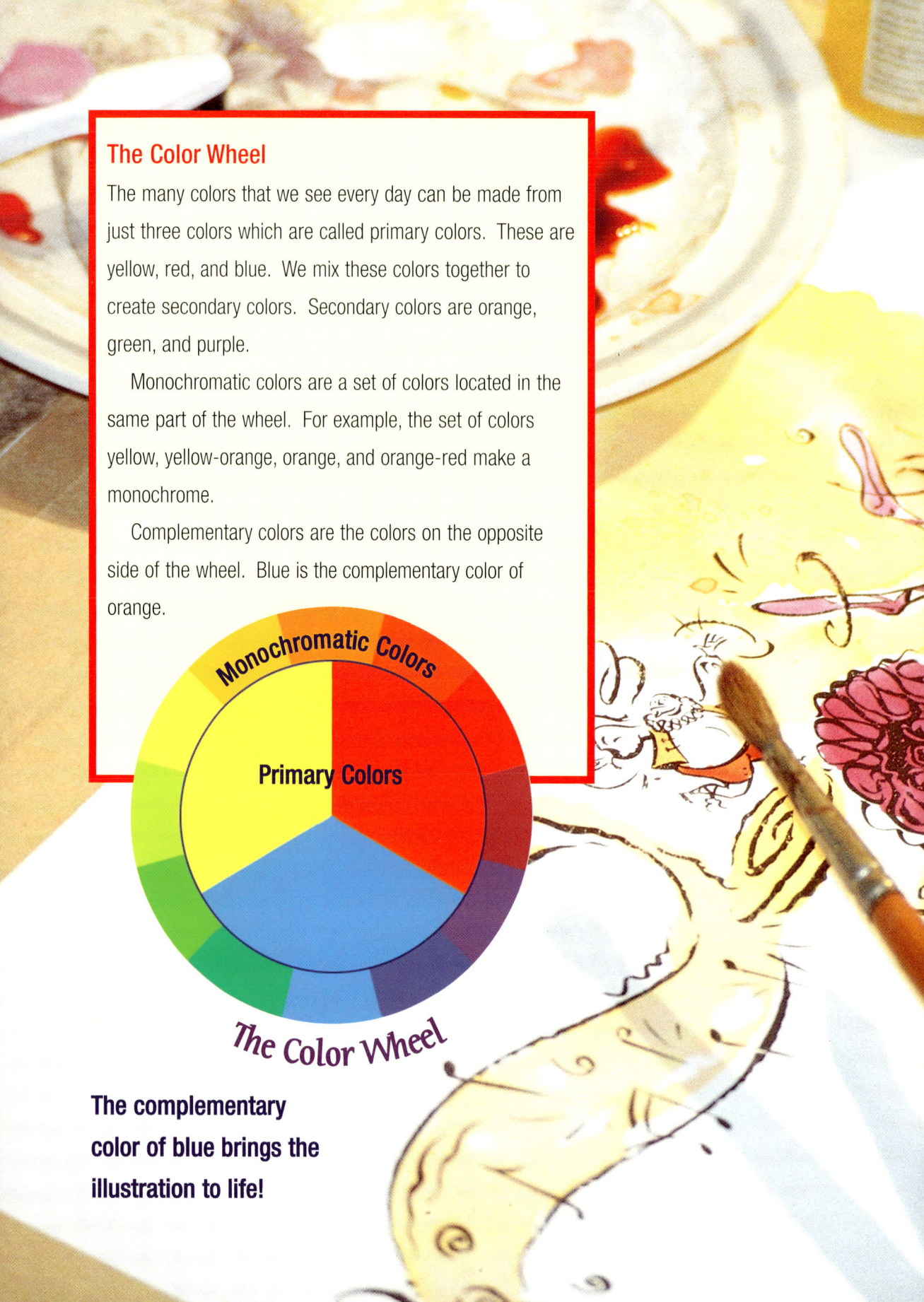

The Color Wheel

The complementary color of blue brings the illustration to life!

When the paper with the photocopied outlines is dry, I splash the color on. I have been careful with the outlines, so I can be loose with the color. I use watercolors and dyes so that my outlines still show through. I don't mind if color goes over the lines.

For this illustration, free use of color adds to the feeling of movement. I use wet brushes and wash lots of bright monochromatic colors into the background to give a feeling of stage lights. I even use a toothbrush to splatter the color around, adding to the atmosphere of movement, light, and excitement.

The illustration is mainly orange in color, so I use the complementary color of blue to add highlights. This really brings the illustration to life.

When the paint has dried, I use chalk pencils and a fine black pen to add any details that should be emphasized. I notice that I need to redraw the outline of Walter's shoes, add a rosy color to his cheeks, and add color for the bruises on his arms and legs.

There! This illustration is finished. But I still have ten more to finish and only two days to go! I must work quickly if I am to meet my deadline.

From pencil rough to final art, this illustration is complete.

Computer Illustration

Some illustrators now prefer to use computer software to draw pictures. Instead of paint, brushes, and pencils, they use only a mouse! With computers, illustrators can do almost any style of illustration—and mistakes are much easier to erase!

Finally, all the illustrations are complete. I carefully cover them with a protective sheet of paper and pack them up for delivery to the publisher. I phone the courier company who will deliver my package to the publisher by tomorrow morning. I have made the deadline!

The next day I receive a call from the publisher. They love the illustrations. Hooray! I send an invoice to them so I can get paid. The job is finished.

How Do I Get Paid?

Payment for a service is made after the client has received an invoice from the supplier. In this case, the service is the illustration work and the supplier is the illustrator.

An invoice is a record for both the client and illustrator of the job completed. It requests payment of the agreed fee and can also include added costs that the client has agreed to pay, such as couriers and materials.

Some invoices will also record the time spent on a job and the rate per hour for that time. An invoice will usually request payment within a certain period of time.

Three months later, I receive a copy of the book. It looks great! It is quite strange to see all of my pictures in a finished book—they have been checked, scanned, filmed, and printed since they were delivered to the publisher!

Now, where is that other illustration brief? Hmm, twelve illustrations needed by Tuesday. Better get back to work!

An Illustration Timeline

Week 1
The brief.

Weeks 1–2
Pencil roughs.

Week 3
Client approves roughs.

Weeks 4–6
Final artwork.

Week 7
Artwork delivered.

Week 8
The check!

Index

brief 10, 11, 31
characters 12, 13, 16, 17
colors
    complementary 26, 27
    monochromatic 26, 27
    primary 26
    secondary 26
composition 16, 17, 18
computers 29
contract 11
deadline 11, 28, 30
fax 22, 23
final illustrations 22, 24
information 9
invoice 30
layout 10, 11
pencil roughs 12, 16, 22, 24
perspective 19, 21
portfolio 7, 10
safety 15
studio 14–15
style 6, 7, 9, 10, 18
symbols 9
technique 6, 7, 24
tools 6, 14–15, 24
vanishing point 19
watercolor
    paper 25
    paints 27

Bookweb Links

More Bookweb books
about art and illustration!

Juliette, The Modern Art Monkey—Fiction
The Grumpy Millionaire—Fiction
The Mammoth Hunters—Fiction
Book Steps—Nonfiction
Magnificent Masks—Nonfiction

Key To Bookweb Fact Boxes
☐ Arts
☐ Health
☐ Science
☐ Social Studies
☐ Technology